DPE

DREAM - PLAN - EXECUTE

JOURNAL

By Joshua Ridock King Keller

PURPOSE

"To find your purpose, you must go below the surface"

Many of us have been raised to look for solutions from other sources, typically external, or outside of ourselves. We attend parties to find more joy, we attend religious centers of worship to find peace and inspiration, which is fine, but many of us have spent much of our lives unaware of the power we have within. Just as the gym makes our bodies stronger, life's challenges make us stronger mentally and spiritually. We then see our mental and spiritual muscles grow. When we are in tune with this concept, we may find it easier to identify those things that we are passionate about.

1. Name 5 things you are passionate about.
2. Explain why you are passionate about these things.
3. How can you utilize these 5 passions to help others as well as provide financially for yourself and family?

PRINCIPLES/PHILOSOPHIES

"You will only go as far as who you are"

I remember talking with one of my great mentors some years ago, Fred Whiten, and I explained to him my goals of becoming a millionaire. One of his responses was "I know you can do it" but the other response was "You will only go as far as who you are." His point was that before I could reach that level there were some things about myself that would require some type of change, whether it was my outlook on finances, my relationships with others, etc.

1. What are some things within your principles or philosophies that may need some fine tuning?
2. Do you believe these things are hindering your growth (explain why or why not?)
3. What major shift will you make within the next 30 days that will help you reach an important goal?

PERSEVERANCE

"The doubters will be cruel, so use it as your fuel"

Some of the best success stories have come from those who had the odds stacked against them and/or people who simply did not believe in them. When I was held back in the 6th grade it was a reality check for me. I could sense the disappointment from my mother. I was being considered a "conduct disorder kid." I could tell by her conversation with her friends and her cousin that she was a bit embarrassed to mention me. Some of my family members began to have doubts about me. The following year, I was transferred to a new school. I made a decision that I will never fail again. I made honor roll my first year. I really defied the odds when I was accepted to 4 out of the 5 colleges that I applied for and then graduated college from one of them, then went on to receive paralegal certification, and ultimately my masters degree.

We will always have doubters and life will most certainly offer its share of challenges, but the key is to persevere.

1. What are some of the challenges you currently face?
2. How do you plan to overcome these challenges?
3. What positive change will you make in your life that will help you reach the next level?

PROTECTION

"Your life will reflect the things you protect"

I once heard motivational speaker Eric "ET" Thomas say he doesn't allow people who aren't positively energetic to communicate with him before 1pm. I thought to myself, "This is how important it is for this man to protect his energy and his spirit"

Motivational speaker Tony Robbins often speaks about "asset allocation" or how to wisely use your money so that it grows. He also emphasized protecting your money by making sound decisions, by investing in things that will provide you the best chance of having a good return on investment.

It is very important to protect your assets, whether it is money, business, property, relationships, or your peace of mind.

1. What are some assets that you protect?
2. How do you protect those assets?
3. How does the protection of these assets benefit you and others?
4. Identify a daily routine that you will practice to protect your assets.(Peace of mind/energy, money, property, business/ organization, relationships)

PROCESS

"It won't happen overnight; sometimes
it'll take all 12 rounds of the fight"

As a kid I remember watching the Mike Tyson fights. My face would be glued to the T.V. as he pummeled his opponent like nothing I've ever seen before. We all wanted to fight like Mike Tyson; he would knock out his opponents early in the fight. As I continued to study his fights I noticed something. I noticed that the longer the fight lasted the more Mike Tyson would find himself in trouble, and the better chance his opponent had to beat him. His opponents knew that if they could at least survive the first 7 rounds their chances of winning increased significantly.

The fight may seem tough and the task daunting, but how are you preparing yourself to win against all odds? The victory is much sweeter when the obstacle appears insurmountable, which means the bigger the challenge the greater the reward, but, you must trust the process.

1. List 5 goals that you are going to achieve this year. (Briefly explain how achieving each goal will benefit you or others.)
2. For each goal identify at least one person who will hold you accountable.(Could be same person for multiple goals, if you are that confident in him/her)

DIRECTION

"When the drive is there, and the destination is clear,
you will dodge the potholes depending upon
how well you steer"

Think of the greatest athletes in sports they all have or had two main goals in mind. 1. Be the greatest they could be at their position 2. Win a championship. They have a direction; they put in hours of training even after the mandatory workouts and practices. Let's think of all of the distractions these athletes attract: drugs, negative peers, leaching family members, bad business deals, groupies, etc. These athletes have to remain extremely focused in order to dodge these "potholes" and reach their destinations or goals.

1. Are you giving 100% everyday? (If not, why not?)
2. Are your goals in line with your principles? Elaborate.
3. Identify 3 distractions that you are currently facing?
4. How will you overcome these distractions, and how will you avoid them in the future?

DURABILITY

"When the storm hits will your plan withstand, or will it fall down and sink in the quicksand"

When I served as Chief Service Officer (CSO) for the city of Allentown Pennsylvania we would have these weekly phone conferences with AARP and NYC Mayor Bloomberg's "Cities of Service" reps. There were various CSO's from across the country. One of the ongoing themes or word that I would hear repeated often in almost every meeting was "sustainability."

Our job as the CSO was to create and develop volunteer initiatives and projects that would increase volunteerism within the city. It wasn't enough to create the plan itself, but we also had to understand how the plan would have an impact over the years to come, and how it would be sustained.

1. How sustainable or durable is your plan on a scale of 1-10?
2. Create a 5 year projection. What will you put in place to sustain the lifespan of your plan?
3. What relationships could you build to help benefit your plan?

DIVIDE: Your Time

"Prepare for rain even when days are sunny, wasted time is worse than wasted money"

I often hear successful and or wealthy people discuss how they manage their time very affectively. Time is our most important asset. I remember as I was working on my very first children's book "Nasir Perseveres" my good friend Angelo Goodwin would call and check on me. He would ask, "How is the book coming along" "What is the deadline" "How are you managing your time." He would say "When you don't have a lot of money you must use time to your advantage" My mentor Fred Whiten introduced me to a concept of breaking my days down in quadrants, for example a time outline would look like this 6am-10am, 10am-2pm, 2pm-6pm, 6pm-10pm.

1. How do you manage your time daily?
2. List your weekly priorities for the next 30 days.
3. For the next 30 days create a daily quadrant chart.
4. At the end of the 30 days write down how well or how poorly you performed with regards to staying on task and in sync with the quadrant formula.

DISTANCE

"Sometimes in order for it to grow, you must keep it low"

When you are working on a positive change in your life or manifesting something, you have to distance yourself from certain types of people. Energy is transferrable, so it behooves us to be wise in the selection of our company.

When I am writing a song, a book, or anything, I prefer to be alone, secluded in a room where no one can disturb or distract me. Soldiers who are in the battlefield have a mission to accomplish. They are not allowed to have their family and friends call them directly to speak with them. They are protected from outside distractions. It is important to have the focus and discipline of a soldier, because like them our livelihood depends on it.

1. Identify 3 things (or people) that you must distance yourself from.
2. Develop a daily schedule which includes at minimum 1 hour per day of alone time.
3. Connect with at least 1 positive productive person weekly over the next 30 days. Spend 1 hour communicating or co-developing something.

DEADLINES

"When you have a goal you must never slack, because once you lose time you can never have it back"

I recall working on my paralegal certification. It seemed as if every document was time sensitive. An entire case could sometimes rest on the appropriate or timely filing of a legal document. You could have your grade drop an entire letter grade if it is submitted 24 hours later. What if we applied this same concept to our lives? Treat your goals as if your entire livelihood depends on it, because in reality it does. Priorities are the key; it serves us well when we understand which things in our lives are most important. Your dream is like your court case, and just like legal filings each goal in between must be achieved in a timely fashion.

1. For each goal that you listed on the "Process" page you will create a realistic timeline to achieve these goals. (Check off goals as you go)
2. What adjustment or changes if any have you made?
3. Check in with person holding you accountable with your goal. (Weekly conference calls or meetings recommended)

EDUCATION

"Sometimes the amount you earn, is directly correlated with what you learn"

Let's take a moment and think about the brain surgeon profession. Relatively speaking brain surgeons make pretty good money. The brain surgeon has to attend school longer than the "regular" doctor. The brain surgeon has to specialize in his/her area. This requires additional education which then equals an increase in salary or net worth.

Some of us want to "get rich" really quickly. This is the reason we gamble at the casinos, purchase lottery tickets, etc. However, it is education and self-education that will help us not only acquire the things we want, but also maintain them. It behooves us to learn as much as possible the industry that we are passionate about. It also benefits us to understand ourselves as well as the psychology and behavior of others.

1. Identify a subject or area that you will study for the next 30days. (List 3 ways that it will benefit you or your business).
2. Find one person in this area who will be interested in mentoring you.(Establish a healthy relationship with this person)
3. Identify at least one person who could benefit from having you as their mentor.

ELEVATION

"Before reaching your wealth,
you must see value in being yourself"

Becoming wealthy is a process. The mind and the spirit are the first things that must change in order to reach higher levels in life. If you have an impoverished mind-state or spirit it wouldn't matter if someone gave you a million dollars, it's likely you will end up broke again within 365 days. When we elevate our mind and spirit we offer a greater benefit to ourselves and others. This change is a process. It is important that we learn and practice certain principles, such as self love before we obtain material success. Without knowledge and understanding of this concept the monetary/material gain could be like poison as we may literally kill ourselves trying to become happy. Perhaps, we should learn a bit about our history and/or cultural heritage as well as that of others. It is imperative that we identify and acknowledge our higher self, as we first recognize ourselves as kings and queens before anyone else does. We must know that we are worthy of every blessing that we acquire.

1. For the next 30 days look at yourself in the mirror in the morning and speak a positive affirmation beginning with "I AM"
2. Once a week, do something kind for someone (Please be genuine in your efforts).
3. Change something in your diet and exercise routine. (Pick one unhealthy food that you will stop eating) (Exercise at least twice a week, if you already exercise regularly challenge yourself with a weight loss or strength gain goal)

EVALUATION

"Never lose track of your progress, know your worth or you will be given a lot less"

There was a woman who worked a job as a nurse for 2 years. Before she was officially hired she was given a dollar amount that she would be paid hourly. She was told that she would receive a raise after 6 months, but on the 7th month, no raise! She remained patient and thought "maybe I'll get my raise after 1 year instead of the 6 months." She worked harder than she had ever worked, and before she knew it another 6 months had passed, which meant that 1 year had gone by since she was hired, still she received no raise! She promised herself that she would give the job 1 more year of her life and if she did not receive a raise she would then quit! 2 years had passed since her hiring date. She was extremely bothered as she walked into her manager's office and stated "I have been here for 2 years why haven't I been given a raise" Her manager asked "How much of a raise should you get" She replied at least $5 dollars per hour ($10,400 annually in raise). He then replied "How do we know how much you deserve, you have never received an evaluation"

No matter where you are in the process, always remember to evaluate your progress.

1. On a scale of 1-10, how aligned with your purpose are your goals? What can you do to make that rating higher (if lower than 9), or how can you sustain your rating if it is currently 9 or 10?

EXECUTE

2. Reflecting on your goals and your plan, are there any shortcomings or inconsistencies that you or the person holding you accountable have noticed? If yes, what are they, and what can you do to become better?
3. Are you and at least one other person holding you accountable consistently? Get constructive criticism from them in regards to your progress (meet in person or hold a 15 minute conference call)
4. Refer to your "Divide: Your Time" page. How are you doing with your time management? What can you do to better prepare you for the execution of your plan?

EVOLUTION

"Wins and losses, I have received both, as they were major contributors to my growth"

I have learned that perseverance is a key component to becoming successful. My good friend and fellow Philadelphia native Nehemiah Davis always tells the story about how he was fired from numerous jobs, kicked out of schools and still managed to turn things around for the positive. He started his journey by simply selling fruit from a fruit truck and also serving the less fortunate. He now runs his own foundation the "Nehemiah Davis Foundation." He won the 2016 "Steve Harvey Neighborhood Award" and has a successful company called the "Circle of Greatness Academy" (COGA), amongst other accolades.

Would there have been any of this success if Nehemiah had not changed and evolved from the days of being fired from jobs and kicked out of schools? That's probably highly unlikely. I recall having a phone conversation with Nehemiah back in 2013 and I was becoming a bit discouraged by the lack of support I was receiving for the things I was doing such as my music and event hosting, etc. Frustrated, I complained and said "Maybe I should just forget it and do something else" his response was rather clear and concise he said "Whether you do it or not, it's your dream and no one else's, the only person you would hurt is you"

EXECUTE

What I took away from that conversation was invaluable. You will have wins and losses in life, and sometimes the losses will seem more prevalent than the wins, but it is your job to persevere and develop a winning spirit no matter what! This dream and plan that you are preparing to execute belongs to you and no one else.

1. Develop a daily routine of prayer and/or meditation
2. Remembering why you started this journey, develop 3 coping techniques that you will utilize when thoughts of doubt or times of discouragement occur. (What are 3 ways that you will manage to overcome mental or circumstantial challenges?)
3. How often are you exercising? Increase exercise routine to a minimum of 3 days per week until you are able to exercise consistently at 5 days per week. There is a mind – body – spirit connection. Document the changes that you are experiencing (mental, physical, spiritual) as you continue on your fitness journey.
4. While interacting, speak at least one positive affirmation over a minimum of 1 person's life or circumstance at least once daily. (Do this for the next 14 days, and document any positive change that you notice).

EXECUTION

"The only way to make it happen is by taking action"

One of my mentors Donald Clayton, retired military veteran, and real estate investor had his sights set on an investment property, he bid on the property and then purchased the investment property. When he purchased the property, he told me how much work he would need to put into it in order to bring it up to the standard of the vision he had for it. So, then he spent thousands of dollars on renovations so that he would benefit from the after-repair value (ARV). Months went by and finally the house was fixed up and ready to be sold to a buyer. We were on another phone call and he mentioned his new "problem" the property was finished and ready to sell, but he has not been able to find a buyer. Here he is in a situation where he spent loads of money purchasing and fixing this place and now, he has to sit on the property essentially losing money, because his intention is to sell and not rent, which means he is not making money from rental to cover expenses. Although this seemed like a "major" problem he remained calm because he had taken action when he bought the property and was prepared for whatever the consequences. Finally, after roughly one year since purchasing the property he was able to sell it and still make a profit. Had he not taken action when he had his sights set on this property, he would have never had the property to sell in order to make a profit to begin with.

Some of the people who I have mentioned such Nehemiah Davis and Donald Clayton have one thing in common they did not allow their dreams to remain a dream. They developed a plan and they executed until those dreams came to fruition. Do not wait, you have what it takes. You are probably a bit nervous and apprehensive, but that is not uncommon. This is your time. All you have to do is Dream, Plan, and Execute!

To help you a bit further I have developed a brief game plan that you may find useful:

7 POINT EXECUTION PLAN

1. Identify your target audience. Provide sample of product to targeted group. Collect participants contact information.
2. Establish newsletters and develop surveys, get feedback. (Recommended - www.constantcontact.com).
3. Establish social media platform.
4. Host or participate in events, video conferences, and other mediums that will afford interaction with others and exposure.
5. Film events, photograph product, record short commercials (YouTube).
6. Establish healthy relationships (Notice I didn't say network!).
7. Evaluate and make necessary adjustments.

Believe in yourself, get out of this journal and make things happen!

Dream Plan Execute

Joshua "Ridock King" Keller is a book author, writer, entrepreneur, and founder of Dream Plan Execute LLC. Born in Philadelphia, PA "Ridock King" relocated to Atlanta, GA where he successfully founded and operates several businesses. He is also involved in the community dedicating time to feeding the homeless, and hosting free entrepreneurship, financial literacy, and self-empowerment classes for the youth. He is a creative who knows that his gifts were given so that he can help others identify their gifts and live up to their full potential. When he is not reading and writing books, creating short film projects, building his businesses, and spending time with family he is writing music that people can feel and that will positively impact the lives of those who listen and relate to it.

Although, he has multiple college degrees he knows and understands that entrepreneurship is the backbone of financial freedom. The foundation of any positive success is adherence to principles. These same principles must help improve the family, community, and society in some way. This journal is designed to help improve individuals, families, communities, and ultimately society.

Joshua "Ridock King" Keller can be found online:

www.iamridockking.com
www.dreamplanexecutebooks.com
www.dreamplanexecutestore.com
www.dreamplanexecute.com
@ridockking
@dream_plan_execute
@nasirperseveres

www.ingramcontent.com/pod-product-compliance
Lightning Source LLC
LaVergne TN
LVHW061226100826
845148LV00004B/878

* 9 7 8 1 7 3 6 0 1 0 1 2 9 *